The Holy Spirit:
Same Person,
Two Distinct Works

The Holy Spirit:
Same Person,
Two Distinct Works

Pastor Olivia Daniels

 iUniverse®

The Holy Spirit: Same Person, Two Distinct Works

iUniverse books may be ordered through booksellers or by contacting:

iUniverse
1663 Liberty Drive
Bloomington, IN 47403
www.iuniverse.com
1-800-Authors (1-800-288-4677)

ISBN: 978-1-5320-0634-0 (sc)
ISBN: 978-1-5320-0633-3 (e)

Library of Congress Control Number: 2016914717

Print information available on the last page.

iUniverse rev. date: 10/07/2016

Dedication

I dedicate the book, *The Holy Spirit: Same Person, Two Distinct Works* to all believers everywhere, whose thoughts may be similar to my old thoughts before the infusion of the Holy Spirit. I ask that you invite him into your heart, so the second work, can be empowered with boldness and authority for the effectiveness of the kingdom of God. He longs to be enthroned in your heart and to use you as a vessel in the earth's realm for His Glory. God has given us his word and spirit to equip us with what we need to run this race. Let's run in complete victory!

Contents

Dedication vii

Acknowledgement.. xi

Introduction   The Fullness in the Holy Spirit.............. xiii

Chapter I   The Trinity: God the Father, God
                the Son, God the Holy Spirit 1

Chapter II   Salvation 4

Chapter III   The Holy Spirit is a Person........................ 6

Chapter IV   Regeneration: Indwelling of the
                Holy Spirit 9

Chapter V   Why We Need the Holy Spirit................11

Chapter VI   Transformation 15

Chapter VII   Invitation to be Infused by
                the Holy Spirit: Two Distinct Works........19

Chapter VIII   Love.. 24

Chapter IX   Forgiveness................................. 26

Chapter X   Prayer.. 29

Testimony 31

Glossary According to Strong's Concordance
(Hebrew) by James Strong...............................35

Scriptures 39

Notes 45

Acknowledgement

I first give thanks to my Lord Jesus Christ, who is my savior above all else, without the Holy Spirit guidance and unction I could never had taken on such a task. I do not take it lightly as I pen His Holy word to the believers and unbelievers. Thank you Lord for this privilege to honor you. To my daughters, Felicia Daniels and Bridgette Daniels, I thank them for their support, prayers, and encouraging words when I could not see the end of the tunnel.

I thank my family and co-laborers for their encouragement, for standing in the gap for me when I became weary, declaring and decreeing the word of God over his gifts inside of me until it was birth.

A special thanks go out to Sister Hope Sutton a special sister in the Lord, who did not think it was robbery to voluntarily give up her time to bless someone else with her gifts as an editor. Without you, this book may still be waiting in the wind to be propelled. I am forever grateful for your gift being a blessing to me. May God return your blessing 100 hundred fold back to you.

To my sister and Pastor, Gertrude Corbett, thank you as a visionary, of Alpha and Omega Ministries of Deliverance, in Brooklyn, New York, for always being there for me. I'm so grateful for your prayers that keeps me anchored,

Thank you iuniverse, Publishing, for all of your support.

Introduction

The Fullness in the Holy Spirit

Has there ever been a thought in your heart or head that there's more to being save than being saved? For me, the thought of accepting Jesus was somehow incomplete. I mean it felt right knowing that if I had died right then, I would have been with the Lord in paradise? Years had passed and my inner man continued to search for the missing piece. I continued to read God's word and meditate on it, I even got involved with Bible study groups. However, my soul continued to thirst and my heart still beat for more. Did I mention I was not the first one in my family to be saved and baptized in the Holy Spirit? My oldest brother, Bennie was the first to surrender his heart and bad habits, and years later my sister Gertrude, who surrendered to Jesus in total submission. But even though I was not the first to get saved, I was the first to find a church home. And yet I was still not fully committed. As for me, I was still holding out. Right here, I must give Jesus a Shout of Praise! *He waited for me!* And when I was ready to come to Him just as I was, a sinner, lost, and in need of a savior, there *He was waiting for me!* As mentioned in the above sentences, my heart was not satisfied so I pursued Him even more and found the missing piece.

John 14:26 states that the Helper, who is the Holy Spirit, whom the Father will send in my name will teach you all things, and bring to your remembrance all that I said to you. In this verse, John is still proclaiming that the Holy Spirit is a counselor, helper, intercessor, advocate, and a strengthener. Folks, there's no way around this. We need the spirit of God to live holy. The Holy Spirit is the person that keeps us from living an unrighteous life style. When we want to do wrong we just can't, when we want to return back to our sin, we just can't do it. What is stopping us from returning to that old man? The Holy Spirit.

Jesus tells Nicodemus in John 3:3-5, that he must be born again and why. Unless you are born again, you can never enter into the kingdom of God. So if that was true for Nicodemus, it's true for us. We truly need the third person of the trinity for our new life in Christ. *Jesus said I am the way, the truth, and the life; no man cometh unto the Father but by me (John 14:6).* Contrary to what others may think, "there is no other way we can come to the Father except through His son Jesus Christ." Some people believe other doctrine and think that there are many roads to heaven. Sorry to have to tell you but that just isn't true. There is one truth and that truth is written in the *Holy Bible.* Reading the Bible and asking the Holy Spirit for revelation, is how we begin to grow and become true disciples of Jesus Christ. We then understand whose we are and who we are in Christ. To know who we belong to on this journey in life is vital to our lifestyle children of God. If we don't know Jesus as Savior, who can save anyone, or as a strong tower who is all powerful, then we can't possibly know that he wins not some battles, but every battle. My fight was always with the flesh, until one day the Holy Spirit revealed to me in *Ephesians 6:12, "For we wrestle not against flesh and blood, but against principalities, against powers, against the rulers of the darkness of this world, against spiritual wickedness in high places" (KJV)*. There was a time in my life when I didn't know that. But I know it now. He *reigns* with all power in His hand.

Chapter I

The Trinity:
God the Father, God the Son,
God the Holy Spirit

The Trinity exists as three persons in one, God the Father, God the Son, and God the Holy Spirit. The Bible clearly speaks of the three as stated above. If we were to use math, it would be 1+1+1=3. God is a triune God. The term Tri meaning three, Unity meaning one, together equals Trinity. God is three persons who have the same essence of deity. As stated in *Trinity of the Church Fathers,*

"According to this central mystery of most Christian faiths, there is only one God in three persons, 'It is the Father who generates, the Son who is begotten, and the Holy Spirit who proceeds', and in their relations with one another, they are stated to be one in all else, co-equal, co-eternal, and consubstantial, and each one is God, whole and entire."[1]

The Father and the Son and the Holy Spirit are not names for different parts of God, but one name for God because three persons exist in God as one entity. They cannot be separated from one another. Here are a few scriptures that show God as one, God as Trinity:

Hear, O Israel! The Lord is our God, the Lord is one! (Deuteronomy 6:4).

There is no God but one (1 Corinthians 8:4).

And after being baptized, Jesus went up immediately from the water; and behold, the heavens were opened, and he saw the Spirit of God descending as a dove, and coming upon Him, and behold, a voice out of the heavens, saying, "This is My beloved Son, in whom I am well pleased (Matthew 3:16-17).

Go therefore and make disciples of all nations, baptizing them in the name of the Father and the Son and the Holy Spirit (Matthew 28:19).

Jesus said: "I and the Father are one" (John 10:30).

He who has seen Me has seen the Father (John 14:9).

He who beholds Me beholds the One who sent Me" (John 12:45).

The Holy Spirit is a member of the Godhead. He has no beginning and no end. The Holy Spirit dwells in earth in every believer's heart. Throughout the Bible, we can see the Holy Spirit pouring out his power and gifts onto the followers of God.[2] Paul, who wrote the book of Corinthians states that there are different kinds of gifts, but the same spirit.

"To one there is given through the Spirit the message of wisdom, another the message of knowledge, to another faith, by the same spirit gifts of healing, working of miracles, to another prophecy, discernment of spirits, to another different kinds of tongues, and to another interpretation of tongues" (1 Corinthians 12:8-10).

According to the Bible all of these are the work of one and the same spirit, and he gives them to each one, just as he determines.[3] These gifts work in the church for the benefit of the church. Those in a relationship with Jesus Christ should have a different way of thinking. When we're transformed our thoughts should be different from the world's in making decisions. This transformation can only be done by the Holy Spirit. When you receive salvation and ask the Holy Spirit to come into your heart, He fills you and dwells in your heart, he becomes your truth and your counselor. Jesus said, "I tell you the truth, it is expedient for you that I go away, and if I go not away, the Comforter will not come unto you; but if I go, I will send him unto you.

Chapter II

Salvation

Our relationship begins with accepting Jesus Christ as the son of God and inviting Him into our hearts to save us. *Romans 10:9 declares that if you confess with your mouth, Jesus is Lord, and believe in your heart that God raised him from the grave, you will be saved.* This was Jesus purpose for coming and dying on the cross for our sins. So that we may live again with Him. Here is one of my favorite verses, *"For everyone who calls on the name of the Lord will be saved"*, *(Romans 10:13).* How good is our Savior? It is then that the Holy Spirit who fills us and becomes the teacher that directs us into the word of truth.

In the beginning there may be struggles and it's okay because Jesus already knows forehand about all of our short comings. This is the reason why He sent the Holy Spirit to be our guide. The Bible declares we are sealed with the Holy Spirit until the day of redemption,[4] and nothing can break this seal. The process in which we go through in knowing Jesus as our Lord and Savior is not a religion, but an authentic relationship. It's getting to know Him for yourself and not by the many voices that you hear in the atmosphere. Building a relationship with God allows us to keep our focus on His word. We lay our affection and praise before Him as a sacrificial offering. We present our daily lives and lace them before God as an offering and He then transforms our lives by making us more like him. Salvation is free, there's nothing we've done to deserve it. *For God so loved the world, that He gave His only begotten Son, and whosoever believeth in Him shall not perish, but have everlasting life (John 3:16).*

The word begotten derives from the Greek word monogenes. According to the Greek-English Lexicon of the New Testament and Other Early Christian Literature (BAGD, 3rd Edition), monogenes have two primary definitions. The first definition is pertaining to being the only one of its kind within a specific relationship.[5] This is the meaning in Hebrews 11:17, when the writer refers to Isaac as Abraham's *only begotten son.*[6] Abraham had more than one son, but Isaac was the only one he had by Sarah and the only son of the covenant. The second definition is pertaining to being the only one of its kind or class, unique in kind.[7] This is the meaning that is implied in John 3:16. There is no other like Jesus. He is unique. *Hallelujah!* So your new birth begins. When we look back at our relationships with parents, spouses, or other family members, can you say that they love us unconditionally, no matter what we do or say?

Chapter III

The Holy Spirit is a Person

Let me begin by saying He is the third person of the Trinity. There is God the Father, God the Son, and God the Holy Spirit. I pray that by the time you finish reading this book that your life is transformed and your relationship with Jesus is brand new or renewed. The Holy Spirit is a member of the Godhead. He has no beginning and has no end with the Father and the Son, he existed before creation. The spirit dwells in the heavens but also on the earth and in the hearts of every believer. Throughout the Bible, we see the Holy Spirit pouring his power into followers of God. When we think of Joseph, Moses, David and Paul, we may feel we have nothing in common with them, but the truth is that the Holy Spirit helped each of them to change, as he will help you to change. The Holy Spirit's name describes his chief attribute. He is perfectly holy and spotless.

The Holy Spirit is free of any sin or darkness. He shares the strength of God the Father and God the Son. He is omnipotent - all-powerful[8], omnipresent – everywhere[9], and omniscient - all knowing.[10,11] Right here is a good place to shout! *Great is our Lord, and mighty in power!* His understanding is infinite.[12] He, both God and the Word (who became Christ) have existed eternally and before all else. From them emanates the Spirit of God who is omnipresent and omniscient. God the Father is the divine Father of the God family into which converted Christians shall be born.[13] Likewise, he is all loving, forgiving, merciful and just.

The first appearance of the Holy Spirit is seen in Genesis 1:2 in the creation, *Now the earth was formless and empty, darkness was over the surface of the deep, and the spirit of God was hovering over the water.* Who is he? He is the one who caused the Virgin Mary to conceive a child.[14] He descended on Jesus like a dove when baptized by John the Baptist.[15] Who is he? He was the one who rested like tongues of fire on the Apostles.[16] He is our inspiration. He inspired men to write the Bible, guides the church, and sanctifies believers in their walk with Christ today - that includes us. He gives spiritual gifts for strengthening the body of Christ. He orchestrates Christ's presence on earth, counseling, and encouraging Christians as they battle the temptations of the world and the forces of Satan. If you are still not sure of who he is. Let's recount. *1.* He is all knowing, all seeing, all powerful. He knows what you are doing and thinking at all times. 2. He is the third part of the Trinity. 3. He is breath and wind.[17] 4. He is the giver of spiritual gifts for the edifying of the church, a counselor when we need advice or directions, a teacher that teaches us all things we need to know, a discerner of truth, he lets us know when someone is being truthful or not, he is a revealer of all scripture. He is holy and spotless, free of sin and darkness, comforter when troubles come our way. He'll walk with us through the darkest moments of your life, give us peace, and convicts us of our sins. He is an intercessor in prayer for you when you don't know what to pray. The Holy Spirit is a keeper. He keeps us from all harm and danger. Lastly, He is the one that calls us into ministry. He tells us our assignments for the purpose of the kingdom of God. Isn't He awesome? How can we live without him? Through the Holy Spirit we are restored to paradise, led back to the kingdom of heaven and adopted as His children. We are given the confidence to call God "Father" and to share in Christ's grace. We are called children of light and given a share in eternal glory. God is all of that and so much more! Receiving Jesus in your heart and walking with the Holy Spirit to perform the will of the Father offers us a promised gift from the Father. Now that you've received a greater revelation of who the Holy Spirit is, does this sound like someone you might want to know and have as a friend forever?

Chapter IV

Regeneration: Indwelling of the Holy Spirit

In Joel 2:28-29[18] and Matthew 3:11[19] we see the baptism in the Holy Spirit. The fulfillment of that promise is described as being filled with the Holy Spirit. The baptism in the Holy Spirit and receiving the Holy Spirit at regeneration are different. Regeneration is a recreation and transformation of the person by the Holy Spirit. Here is what happens. One that is born again cannot make sin a habitual practice in their lives, you cannot remain born again without a sincere desire to please God and avoid evil.[20], God himself imparts eternal life in us and you become a child of God,[21,22] a new person. You no longer conform to this world[23] but are now created to be like God in true righteousness and holiness.[24] This is necessary because apart from Christ, all people, in their inherent nature are sinners, incapable of obeying and pleasing God.[25,26] Eternal life comes to those who repent of sin, turn to God and put their faith in Jesus Christ as Lord and Savior. Right here, you are probably thinking, so that's the reason I can't live a holy and righteous life… because I'm not connected to the source. Just keep on reading and keep an open mind. It starts with a new birth. Regeneration is a transition from an old life of sin to a new life of obedience to Jesus Christ.[27,28]

In other words, the things you use to do you no longer wish to do them because of your new love for Christ.

You know longer have that same desire to follow after the things in this world, but a spiritual desire to obey God and follow after the leading of the Holy Spirit. Just as one can be born of the Spirit by receiving the life of God, he or she can also extinguish that life by ungodly choices and unrighteous living, and therefore die spiritually. Scripture affirms in *Romans 8:13 that, if you live according to the sinful nature, you will die.* You cannot remain born again without a sincere desire to please God. This is only accomplished through the grace given to believers by Christ Jesus, and through a dependence on the Holy Spirit *(Romans 8:2-14).*

Chapter V

Why We Need the Holy Spirit

I don't know about you, but I need the Holy Spirit in my life because He keeps me from sinning against God when my flesh buffets against my spirit. Paul puts it like this, *when I want to do right evil is present with me, (Romans 7:21).* He gives us the strength to resist the devil and causes him to flee from you (James 4:7). *We as Christians must first submit ourselves to God and then resist the devil.* The Holy Spirit helps us to submit to God the Father and the Son and then he strengthens us to withstand or oppose the devil and his tricks. We need the Holy Spirit to help us recognize the truth when we are being tempted to sin against God. The Holy Spirit is a discerner of the truth. He is the one that tells us the difference between truth and untruth. *John 10:10 Jesus says the thief comes to steal, kill, and destroy. I have come that we may have life and have it more abundantly.* He the Holy Spirit, shows up and save us from making the biggest mistakes in our life. Often times we may find ourselves saying something like this, "Something told me not to go that way", or "put my money in that IRA." Now are you beginning to see why we need more and more of Him every day of our life? Sometimes in our lives, mistakes we make for not being wise can cause us great sorrow. But if we invite the Holy Spirit to take control of us in the same manner as he did when he filled the prophets with the word of God, He'll do the same for us. The Bible declares the Spirit of God, who raised Christ from the dead, lives in you. And just as he raised Christ from the dead, he will give life to your mortal body by this same spirit living within you.[29] What does all that mean? This means **He's Got Us!** He raises us so we can see the trickery of the enemy and not fall in his trick bag. He is the one that gives life and raises us up in the power of God Almighty. I hope it is becoming clearer to you why we need him so.

Even while I write, I pray the Holy Spirit will open your eyes and raise you up right now. I pray that where you were once blind, *now* you see! *Praise God for His great love!*

We also need the Holy Spirit to transform us so we won't be conformed to this world. *Romans 12:2 says, "And be not conformed to this world, but be ye transformed by the renewing of your mind, that ye may prove what is that good, and acceptable and perfect, will of God. (KJV).* It's a process. Some people believe that when we are saved and receive Jesus as Lord and Savior, this means we don't have to do anything else. Just wait to go to heaven. Oh Yeah! we're on our way to heaven, saved from the everlasting burning flames. Not completely so! God's transformation, the renewing of our mind is a condition. Yes, you may go to heaven but there is a lot more to it. We are now to learn who we are in Christ and to allow His Word to perform a work in us while we're still here on earth. We must become instruments of God. *II Timothy 2:15 says we must study to show ourselves approved unto God, a workman that needeth not be ashamed, but rightly dividing the word of truth* (KJV). The Amplified version of this scripture puts it this way, *"Study and be eager for nothing and do your utmost to present yourself to God (approved - tested by trial), a workman who has no cause to be ashamed, correctly analyzing and accurately dividing (rightly handling and skillfully teaching) the word of truth."* The Holy Spirit is so skillful and perfect at teaching us things, working in and through us. We need the Holy Spirit to understand how to rightly divide the word and how to walk in the word with authority as we are tested. You would agree that we need Him as a teacher. See, unbelievers view things with their natural eyes and intellect.

There are some who view things with the natural eye and intellect, but for those in Christ Jesus, their thoughts are different. Philippians 4:8 states that we should *fill our mind on things true, noble, reputable, authentic, compelling, gracious- the best. Put into practice what you learned from me, what you have heard and saw and realized.* Do that and God will make everything work together for your good. We need the Holy Spirit to shed light on daily living with Jesus and how we are to receive others. When you first give your life to Christ, you may feel that life is going great for you, but it is important that you stay in the word continually. So read the Bible daily, read all the Christian books you can and The Holy Spirit will teach you how to hear God's voice.

There are many people that read the written word of God without knowing the Holy Spirit. You can brush shoulders with Jesus on every page of the scripture and miss Him when He shows up. The Pharisees did it. They read, taught, and prayed about the Messiah all of their lives. But when He showed up they rejected Him. It is possible that some people who have believed in the Holy Spirit all their lives will not release total control of themselves to Him when He shows up. We have to get close to the Holy Spirit again, to trust. There will be disappointments and challenges in the church, but the Holy Spirit will turn your attention to the *Word* (Jesus) and show you how to press your way through difficult times. If we are going to be witnesses as Christ called us to be, we must have the fullness of the Holy Spirit in our lives in order to walk in the Spirit. We can literally impact the entire world if we allow the Holy Spirit to work in us and if we yield to the fullness of the Spirit.

Chapter VI

Transformation

As you read the different meanings for transformation (conversion, change, alteration, metamorphosis,) consider the Amplified version of Romans 12:2,

do not be conformed to this world (age), but be transformed (changed) by the (entire) renewal of your mind (by its new ideals and its new attitude), so that you may prove (for yourselves) what is the good and acceptable and perfect will of God, even the thing which is good and acceptable and perfect (in his sight for you).

Transforming us is a function of the Holy Spirit, not man. The Spirit conforms us from our old habits and thoughts to Jesus' character. The third part of the Trinity, which His presence within us accomplishes love, peace, patience, temper, kindness, goodness, gentleness, meekness, and humility.[30] If we ask Him into our hearts, and to be Lord over our lives, he will come and dwell there. *Ephesians 3:17 (NLT) says, "Then Christ will make his home in your hearts as you trust him. Your roots will grow down into God's love and keep you strong."* Those in a relationship with Jesus Christ should have a different way of thinking. When we're transformed, our thoughts should be different from the world's in making decisions. This transformation can only be done by the Holy Spirit. When you receive salvation and ask the Holy Spirit to come into your heart, He fills you and dwells in your heart, he becomes your truth and your counselor. Jesus said, "I tell you the truth, it is expedient for you that I go away, and if go not away, the Comforter will not come unto you; but if I go, I will send Him unto you."

Another way of looking at how the Holy Spirit transforms is for us to travel back in time to our third grade science lesson on the stages from caterpillar to butterfly, called metamorphosis. The butterfly has four stages. Each stage is different. Each stage also has a different goal. The life cycle process can take a month to a year:

Stage 1: It starts out as an egg. She lays the egg on a leaf.

Stage 2: This stage is the caterpillar. A caterpillar is sometimes called larva and it looks like a worm. The caterpillar is hungry once it has hatched, so it starts to eat leaves and flowers. It grows so fast that it becomes too big for its skin. The caterpillar shed its skin four or more times while it is growing. It does not say in this stage long.

Stage 3: The caterpillar is done growing and makes a chrysalis or pupa. It is mostly brown or green, typically the same color as its surroundings (trees, leaves, branches). This protects and keeps it from getting hurt. Also known as the changing stage. It then turns into a butterfly.

Stage 4: The adult Butterfly, the last stage in the cycle. The pupa or chrysalis opens and out comes a beautiful colorful butterfly. The butterfly is very tired so it rests when it comes out. After rest, it will be ready to start flying. Rest starts the pumping of the blood into its wings, so their wings will work and flap and learn to fly. It will then find a mate. When it finds a mate, it lays eggs. Then the lifecycle process starts all over again.

This process resembles much of our life when we accept Jesus in our hearts and believe. The Holy Spirit fills us and transform us. Our salvation at that time begins to take root as a seed in our hearts and every day we work to improve it. By the comparison, we see the connection between the first stage of transformation and that moment when Mary had her encounter with the Holy Spirit. He overshadows her and she becomes pregnant with our Savior Jesus Christ.

The second stage of our transformation is the caterpillar stage where we have a cool DNA pattern. In this spiritual stage, we are born again by accepting Jesus as our Savior. *Jesus tells Nicodemus in John 3:3, "Verily, verily, I say unto thee, except a man be born again, he cannot see the kingdom of God."* When we receive Jesus in our hearts and the Holy Spirit fills us, and dwells therein we must allow Him to carry us through the transformation stage. The Holy Spirit is willing if we choose to have Him complete the process of being like Christ Jesus. I mentioned before that a caterpillar sheds its skin four or more times while it is growing. We as believers of Christ shed our skin. We take off the old man and put on the new man by refusing to go to places that the Holy Spirit is not welcome, avoiding unclean movies, searching the internet for wicked and unclean things or making unbelievers our best friend.

The third stage is the chrysalis or pupa. Caterpillars camouflage themselves to look like trees and leaves for protection. As believers in Christ, we never stop growing like the butterfly does, we grow from glory to glory when the Holy Spirit is in charge of our lives. We look to be like our Lord, until our days on this earth are finished. I tell you when we're in this stage of life we desire to become more and more like Jesus. We don't camouflage, *"we just let go and let God,"* He opens us up to become a beautiful butterfly.

Finally, in stage four, we are that beautiful butterfly and we can fly high in Christ Jesus, giving Him praise and worship every day of our lives. And when we fall down and come short of His Glory we will need a refill to move forward into the next season, so the process starts all over, inviting the Holy Spirit to come and infuse us again.

Chapter VII

Invitation to be Infused by the Holy Spirit: Two Distinct Works

There are two distinct works of the Holy Spirit. In John 1:33, Jesus baptizing his believers in the Holy Spirit was to be a sign and dynamic mark of the followers of Jesus. One can be born again and have the Holy Spirit dwell within but still not be baptized in the Holy Spirit.[31] The baptism of the Holy Spirit imparts personal boldness and power into your life in order to accomplish mighty works in Christ's name and to make his witness and proclamation effective.[32,33,34]This is a manifestation of the third part of the trinity in which we first talked about. On that day the impartation of the Holy Spirit by Jesus to his disciples was not the baptism in the Spirit as experienced at Pentecost but rather an infusing of the disciples. Why? For the first time with the regenerating presence of the Holy Spirit and with the new life from the risen Christ, the Holy Spirit was given to the disciples to regenerate, and to make them new creatures in Christ.[35] This receiving of life was the authority of Jesus[36] and their baptism in the Holy Spirit on the day of Pentecost.[37] All believers receive the Holy Spirit at the time of their regeneration and afterwards must experience the baptism in the Spirit for power to be his witness in the earth. *Fulfillment of the Holy Spirit is so important until Jesus instructed his disciples not to begin witnessing until they were baptized in the Holy Spirit and clothed with power from on high (Luke 24:29).* Jesus himself did not enter his ministry until he had been anointed with the Holy spirit and power.[38,39] How much more would we need to be infused by the Holy Spirit after being born again for our promised gift.

We can be baptized (infused) in the Holy Spirit by having a sincere desire to follow Christ and to do His work and to have a hunger and a thirst for righteousness. The first thing is to accept Jesus and the work he has done on the cross for you and receive the indwelling of the Spirit. Second, the Holy Spirit breathes on us to clothe us with power from on high with a show of his glory being manifest with his people. In other words, he seals us with power for service and witness. Jesus is the only one who baptizes His believers in the Holy Spirit with fire for power to witness followed by signs and wonders.

If you could give thought to this scenario it will help you to better understand God's power. You and your friend are crossing the street and a car comes out of no place and strikes your friend and keeps going. He is bleeding profusely from the mouth and his leg is broken, he is near death. Because you are a believer full of the power of God and anointed to do his work, you can perform spiritual CPR before the ambulance arrives. God has given us that power and authority to bind death and speak life into situations and people. *The scripture says that death and life are in the power of your tongue (Proverbs 18:21).* The scripture also says that greater works will you be able to do if you believe on Him and His works (John 14:12). *Stop!* and think about what you have just read and ask the Holy Spirit to infuse you so that this authority and power can belong to you.

Think about the difference it would really make if there were no Holy Spirit in this world. He is the one who keeps the peace here in earth. There wouldn't be any protection, love, power, new birth and even creation. We really need Him in our lives. He is a keeper and a perfect gentleman. If it has been a while since you have had a refilling of God's Spirit and you are not seeing any miracles in your church or family, no one is being set free, and the devil is setting up camp everywhere; take your position in Christ and give the devil an eviction notice. Keep him out of your atmosphere. We know him as a thief, a killer, and a destroyer. He is the father of lies. He is unable to tell the truth. I tell you it sounds as if you need to be refilled with power from on high. Ask the Holy Spirit to breathe on you right now. Confess your sins and ask Him to deliver you and empower you to live according to God's will. Invite him into your life again to do a job that you can't do. Begin to praise the Father for his son Jesus and thank Jesus for redeeming us. It cost you nothing!

I know what you are thinking, I'm too young, I have time. Sorry have to be one to tell you, you don't have time. Do you not see what he's stealing from you, and what he's destroying in your life? He's lying to your parents about each other so that divorce will take place. He's lying to you about marijuana and other drugs, claiming its only for recreation. He's trying to steal your sister's purity by telling her this boy really likes her. Lies, lies and more lies. You're never too young nor too old. Take a look at these extraordinary men in the Bible of whom God chose at an early age in life to work for him. The Bible is full of examples of teenagers called to serve and sacrifice for God. Those who obey God change the course of history. Jeremiah was probably around fourteen when he answered God's call on his life according to some commentary. God did wonderful things for Jeremiah before he was even born. The Bible declares He knew him. He formed him. He set him apart and appointed him as a prophet to the nation.[40] And you know what, He did all of this long before Jeremiah drew his first breath or shed his first tear. Did you know that God chooses us? We didn't choose Him. And I believe He has chosen you, or you would not be reading this book. How beautiful are these words, "*I knew you*"? I made a personal commitment to you even before you were born. If you want to know who you are, you have to know whose you are. Take a moment and chew the fat on these words. Jeremiah started belonging to God as soon as was conceived - like you. And while he was there, God started making preparations for his salvation and ministry - like you. Isn't that amazing? Never should you say "No one loves me" or "I don't know who I am", because God does love you very, much! God has made provision for your life as well and all that you desire or can even think. God has already done it for you.

Daniel was a great prophet, whom God called at 12 years old. David was 25 years old when he was pre-anointed as king over Israel and thirty years old when he was actually anointed as king. In 2 Samuel 5:4 David's life shows us that God is more concerned about a teenager's heart and character than about his talent. God has always trusted youth as significant people, even leaders, who can change the world.

Mary the mother of Jesus was probably between the age of 12 or 14, (there is no scripture that clearly address her age). She gave birth nine months later. Just imagine a teenage bride. Luke 1:28 tell us that she was highly favored. The Virgin Mary was also chosen by God and set apart for God's purpose. Mary was engaged to the carpenter Joseph when she was visited by the angel Gabriel. He told her she would be the mother of the Messiah. You could imagine what was going through Mary's head at that time. But the angel told her how this would happen. Mary was not committing any sin when this pregnancy occurred. The Holy Spirit will come upon you and the power of the Most High will overshadow you; therefore, the child to be born will be called Holy, the Son of God. And it came to pass.

Lastly, Samuel was 12 years old when God spoke to him, and he answered, "Here I am!" this leads us to believe God spoke to Samuel in an audible voice." What a beautiful way to respond to God's word. It isn't that God does not know where we are, but it tells God that we are simply his servants. If God calls your name, will you answer "Here I am!"

Chapter VIII

Love

For God so loved the world, He gave His one and only begotten Son, that whosoever believeth in Him shall not perish but have everlasting life (NIV 3:16). Now that's love. God did not send his son into the world to condemn it, but to save it through him. Jesus demonstrated love from the time he came into this world until his death. He displayed the greatest love any man can show when he suffered a horrific death on the cross. Now that's love! Jesus is as interested in our spiritual birth as he was with Nicodemus. He left his word to reveal regeneration. It is so necessary because apart from Christ all people, in their inherent natures, are sinners, incapable of obeying and pleasing God. Jesus' love for us is immeasurable and unconditional. It is the primary reason why he says you must be born again or we will not see the kingdom of God. No one can enter the kingdom of God unless you are born of water and the spirit. Jesus never leaves us without proper instructions. He tells us how to do it. Jesus gave you free will. Choose this day whom you will serve. Make the right choice. Open up your heart and let love - unconditional love - find a place in your heart today. *Today when you hear his voice, do not harden your heart as Israel did when they rebelled (Hebrews 3:15 NLT).*

Chapter IX

Forgiveness

The Bible speaks about every person needing forgiveness and every person needing to forgive. Why? Because we are all sinners and come short of His Glory. None of us is perfect. We need God's grace and we need to extend that same grace to others. When Jesus died on the cross, He took our punishment upon Himself. He took the guilt of our sins and bore them in our place. He received all the emotional pain, betrayal, abuse, injustice, and scorn that we ourselves have given and received. Read Isaiah 53:5. *Hebrews 9:22 says, under the law, almost everything is purified by means of blood, and without the shedding of blood, there is neither release from sin and its guilt nor the remission of the due and merited punishment for sins.* Jesus paid it all for us on the cross. Look at the cross, think about a man hanging there in your place. A man that knew no sin, left His home in Glory, came down through forty generations, suffered tremendously for us just so you and I could have a second chance to spend eternity with our Creator. We need to understand the cost. He took your place. The punishment for our sin has been paid. Receive what Jesus did for you at Calvary. Repent and change your ways and accept the infusing of the Holy Spirit to shed light on where you are and where you need to go. If you are willing and ready to change, then God is more than ready to help you.

Steps to Receive God's Forgiveness:

- **1John 1:9** *If we confess our sins He will be just to forgive us.*
- **Isaiah 55:7** *Let the wicked forsake his way, and the unrighteous man his thoughts: and let him return unto the Lord, and He will mercy upon him; and he will abundantly pardon.*
- **Hosea 14: 2-3** *Take words with you and return to the Lord. Say to him: forgive all our sins and receive us graciously, that we may offer the fruit of our lips... we will never say 'our gods' to what our own hands have done. The above verses are from the* (NIV)

Put forgiveness in practice…. If you have been wounded, God will take this first. Ration and pain of rejection in your life and work it for something good so you can be a vessel of healing to His people – If you let Him.

- *"But what if they, don't see how bad they hurt me?"*
  - ❖ Whether they see it or not is between them and the Lord. Your responsibility is simply to forgive.

- *"I'm afraid If I forgive, I'll only get hurt again."*
  - ❖ If you call on the Lord for wisdom, He will help you in your situation. If you are in an abusive relationship you need to pray about it.

When God forgives us He no longer holds our sins against us. Therefore; we don't have the right to hold others' sins against them – not if we belong to Jesus. Remember we are blood bought children and we belong to a merciful king. Whether we "feel" forgiveness in our hearts or not, we are under obligation to obey God. As we obey Him, He will supply the feelings. Obedience must come first, then the right feelings will follow.

Chapter X

Prayer

As the Holy Spirit prays through me, I inscribe these words from my heart to yours, I ask you to pray this prayer:

Heavenly Father, God of mercy and grace, I give you my heart today. I pray that you would come and live in my heart. I accept what you did for me on the cross. and I'm thankful for my new birth as a regenerated man/woman/boy/girl, but through the reading of this book, I come to realize that there's something missing in my life. I need the infusing of the baptism of the Holy Spirit. I need your authority and power to be a better witness here in the earth for the kingdom of God. Father breathe on me, so I may be filled with your Spirit and empowered with your authority, like you did the disciples, so that I can be a soul winner for your kingdom. Thank you Lord for receiving me and shedding your blood for me and that I am forgiven for all of my sins. And that I can live with you in paradise.

Testimony

It was 1977 and I was living in Brooklyn, New York. Jesus came into my room and healed me. It is true God did send His word to heal our diseases. I had an infection that the doctors could not identify. It tormented me day and night. Much like the poor man, I cried out to the Lord in distress, He heard me and saved me from all of troubles (Psalm 43:6). That night was when I saw the hand writing on the wall. That night I knew that God was real and like His word says, He is a present helper in the time of trouble. (Psalm 46:1). Here my life began to search for that missing piece I talked about at the beginning of this book. As a born again believer with a renewed mind and indwelling of the Holy Spirit, I assumed I was prepared for anything. Little did I know; I was just half way there. John 10:10 states that the devil comes to steal, kill, and destroy, but I (Jesus) came so that you may have life and have it more abundantly. And that is exactly what happened. I allowed him to steal and destroy my life after Jesus had saved it. You may think that's crazy, but it happened. And it can happen to you too. I was not on the alert and the three warfare brothers deceived me. (lust of the flesh, lust of the eyes and pride of life).[52] Satan tempted me in the areas that Adam and Eve were tempted in. Looking through the eyes of pride I thought what he was offering me was good for me, pleasant to the eyes and a chance for me to be wise. I grabbed for it, not knowing that I had to repay a debt. It's just the opposite with God. He doesn't ask for pay back. He only asks that we love one another as He has loved us. Besides, we can never pay Jesus back for all he has done for us.

My healing was instantaneous! A miracle. So I began studying and reading more and asking God for help. Getting real with God and refraining from being light-hearted with Him, I soon realized He had been waiting on me to come to this point in my life where I would ask Him to draw closer to me. So I began having many conversations with Him which included seeking His face and will for my life.

My husband was military, so we moved to Puerto Rico in 1988. It was at that time that the second phase of the Holy Spirit evolved. Remember the indwelling of the Holy Spirit came when I invited Jesus in my heart and was born again. I want to introduce you to a different work but by the same person. This work is different from when we first received our new birth. The Holy Spirit is the third divine person of the Trinity. He is God's power in action, his active force.[53] It was early one morning, nearly the break of day. I had a dream. I dreamed I was taking a shower. The water was cool and refreshing, nothing like I'd ever felt before. The strangest thing was that I was not in a bathroom as we know a bathroom, but there was inclusiveness. I believed I was being cleansed by the Holy Spirit. As the water sprayed down on me, my entire body felt as if I weighed about 90 pounds. A fat chance that was! The Bible says the Holy Spirit is a cleansing agent, *"Then I will sprinkle clean water on you, and you will be clean; I will cleanse you from all your filthiness and from all your idols" (Ezekiel 36:25).* Also, for this same reason, the baptism of the Holy Spirit is pictured as water being poured out from heaven upon us (Acts 2:17-21). There are many scriptures pertaining to the Holy Spirit and its works. These scriptures vividly describe what I was feeling and seeing. Here are a few:

- **Isaiah 32:15** *Until the Spirit is poured out upon us from on high.*

- **John 13:10** *Jesus answered, "Those who have had a bath need only to wash their feet; their whole body is clean. And you are clean, though not every one of you.*

- **Ephesian 5:25** *Husbands, love your wives, just as Christ loved the church and gave himself up for her*

- **Matthew 8:2** *A man with leprosy came and knelt before him and said, "Lord, if you are willing, you can make me clean."*

- **Matthew 3:11** *I baptize you with water for repentance. But after me comes one who is more powerful than I, whose sandals I am not worthy to carry. He will baptize you with the Holy Spirit and fire.*

As the Holy Spirit gave revelation of my dream, I began to understand what was missing still in my life. I went from being washed by the Holy Spirit to being infused by Him.

(clothe with His power). I desired to be in His presence more and more. To have fellowship and communion with Him. To become His friend and He mine. And He did just that. God wants to use us to tell others about Him. How He saves, forgives all of our sins, heals, delivers, and set us free from the bondage of sin.

So He gives us His spirit to make the job easier and more effective. Because it is not us that's doing the work, it is the greater one that lives inside of us. Here are a few works we find in the Bible concerning the Holy Spirit. He is our guide, discerner of truth, keeper, He convicts when we are doing wrong, sanctifies and purifies.

On that morning in 1988, The Holy Spirit sealed His power in me so I could be His instrument in the earth realm. And guess what! I gave Him a "Yes" and He gave me power to be an effective witness in the earth's realm. And now God is waiting for the others who have not quite made up their mind. I pray that you too will discover the need to be filled and infused with the fire of the baptism in the Holy Spirit. I pray your heart will be filled with a burning desire to have the Spirit of God living and present in you. His purpose is to exalt Jesus and cause you to be an effective witness in the earth for God's Kingdom. Paul who wrote most of the books in the New Testament said, *The Holy Spirit is also a down payment that guarantees that you are completely Christ's, (2 Corinthians 1:22 ESV).*

Glossary According to Strong's Concordance (Hebrew) by James Strong[1]

1. Baptism **of** the Holy Spirit: Describe a movement of the spirit upon or within a believer.

2. Baptism *in* the Holy Spirit: Describe as immersion in or within the spirit of God.

3. Contrite Spirit: (Hebrew- dakka) crushed and broken hearted. Broken down with grief and penitence deeply.

4. Eternity: (Hebrew – olam) long duration. unending or everlasting.

5. Holy Spirit (Hebrew – ruah ha-qodesh) Is the spirit of holiness. Is the third divine person of the trinity; the Triune God manifested as the Father, Son, and the Holy Spirit, each aspect being God.

6. Forgiveness: (Hebrew-salach) to pardon or release someone from an act or debt.

7. Infuse: (Hebrew - zoopoieo) means to empower. To make that which was dead to live, cause to live, quicken.

---

[1] Strong's Concordance Dictionary, by James Strong, published 1890, updated edition KJV 2009: Hendrickson Publisher

8. Intercessor: (Hebrew - Paga) A prayer of petition to God in behalf of another.

9. Iniquities: (Hebrew - avon) crookedness, perverseness. An evil regarded as that which is not straight or upright, moral distortion.

10. Redeem: (Hebrew - gaal) to act as kinsman, revenge, ransom. Released effected by payment of ransom, redemption and deliverance.

11. Regeneration: (Hebrew – paliggenesia) the production of a new life consecrated to God, a radical change of mind for the better. (born again, restoration of life).

12. Ruach: means the wind, breath, or spirit. It first was used in Genesis 1:2, "The spirit of God (Ruach Elohim) was hovering over the waters." In Genesis 6:17 ruach is translated "breath of life." Genesis 8:1 uses ruach to describe the "wind" God sent over the earth to recede the Flood waters.

13. Transformation: (Hebrew – haphak) change, transformed, repent.

14. Salvation: (Hebrew – yesha) to save, rescue, or deliver, to set free.

15. Impartation: (Hebrew – metadidomi) is the giving and receiving of spiritual gifts, blessings, healing, baptism in the Holy spirit.

16. Provision: (Hebrew – tsedah) to provide for.

17. Covenant: (Hebrew – berith) meaning a pact or treaty. An agreement between God and the people of Israel.

18. Pentecost: (Hebrew – shavu'ot) It commemorates God's giving of the Ten commandments at Mount

Sinai. Also Pentecost is recognized as to when the Holy Spirit appeared and brought a miraculous language called tongues, where nations spoke in different languages.

19. Abundant: (Hebrew – marbeh) properly increasing in greatness.

20. Omnipotent: (Hebrew – pantokrato) the quality of having unlimited great power.

21. Omniscience: (Hebrew – El De'ot) The attribute of God known as the all knowing one.

22. Omnipresent: (Hebrew – hippo) means being present everywhere at the same time. Nothing is hidden from Him. (God)

Scriptures

Chapter I: God the Father, God the Son, God the Holy Spirit

2. Acts 8:15-18 15*When they arrived, they prayed for the new believers there that they might receive the Holy Spirit, 16because the Holy Spirit had not yet come on any of them; they had simply been baptized in the name of the Lord Jesus. 17Then Peter and John placed their hands on them, and they received the Holy Spirit.18When Simon saw that the Spirit was given at the laying on of the apostles' hands, he offered them money*

3. **1 Corinthians 12:11** *All these are the work of one and the same Spirit, and he distributes them to each one, just as he determines.*

Chapter II: Salvation

4. Ephesians 4:30 *And do not grieve the Holy Spirit of God, with whom you were sealed for the day of redemption.*

6. **Hebrews 11:17** *By faith Abraham, when God tested him, offered Isaac as a sacrifice. He who had embraced the promises was about to sacrifice his one and only son, (KJV)*

Chapter III: The Holy Spirit is a Person

8. Psalm 147:5 *Great is our Lord and mighty in power; his understanding has no limit.*

9. **Psalm 139:7-10** *Where can I go from your Spirit? Where can I flee from your presence? 8If I go up to the heavens, you are there; if I make my bed in the depths, you are there. 9If I rise on the wings of the dawn, if I settle on the far side of the sea, 10even there your hand will guide me, your right hand will hold me fast.*

10. **Psalm 139:12** *even the darkness will not be dark to you; the night will shine like the day, for darkness is as light to you.*

11. **Hebrews 4:12-13** *For the word of God is alive and active. Sharper than any double-edged sword, it penetrates even to dividing soul and spirit, joints and marrow; it judges the thoughts and attitudes of the heart. 13Nothing in all creation is hidden from God's sight. Everything is uncovered and laid bare before the eyes of him to whom we must give account.*

12. **Psalm 147:5** *Great is our Lord and mighty in power; his understanding has no limit.*

14. **Matthew 1:20** *But after he had considered this, an angel of the Lord appeared to him in a dream and said, "Joseph son*

of David, do not be afraid to take Mary home as your wife, because what is conceived in her is from the Holy Spirit.

15. **Matthew 3:16** *As soon as Jesus was baptized, he went up out of the water. At that moment heaven was opened, and he saw the Spirit of God descending like a dove and alighting on him.*

16. **Acts 2:3** *They saw what seemed to be tongues of fire that separated and came to rest on each of them.*

17. **John 20:22** *And with that he breathed on them and said, "Receive the Holy Spirit.*

Chapter IV: Regeneration: Indwelling of the Holy Spirit

18. Joel 2:28-29 *28"And afterward, I will pour out my Spirit on all people. Your sons and daughters will prophesy, old men will dream dreams, your young men will see visions. 29Even on my servants, both men and women, I will pour out my Spirit in those days.*

19. **Matthew 3:11** I baptize you with water for repentance. But after me comes one who is more powerful than I, whose sandals I am not worthy to carry. He will baptize you with the Holy Spirit and fire.

20. **2 Peter 1:4** *Through these he has given us his very great and precious promises, so that through them you may participate in the divine nature, having escaped the corruption in the world caused by evil desires.*

21. **John 1:12** *Yet to all who did receive him, to those who believed in his name, he gave the right to become children of God*

22. **Romans 8:16** *The Spirit himself testifies with our spirit that we are God's children.*

23. **Romans 12:2** *And be not conformed to this world: but be ye transformed by the renewing of your mind, that ye may prove what is that good and acceptable, and perfect will of God. KJV (Romans 12:2)*

24. **Ephesians 4:24** *and to put on the new self, created to be like God in true righteousness and holiness.*

25. **Psalm 51:5** Surely I was sinful at birth, sinful from the time my mother conceived me.

26. **Jeremiah 17:9** *The heart is deceitful above all things and beyond cure. Who can understand it?*

27. **2 Corinthians 5:17** *Therefore, if anyone is in Christ, the new creation has come: The old has gone, the new is here!*

28. **Galatians 6:15** *Neither circumcision nor uncircumcision means anything; what counts is the new creation.*

Chapter V: Why We Need the Holy Spirit

29. Romans 8:11 *And if the Spirit of him who raised Jesus from the dead is living in you, he who raised Christ from the dead*

will also give life to your mortal bodies because of his Spirit who lives in you.

Chapter VI: Transformation

30. Galatians 5:22 *But the fruit of the Spirit is love, joy, peace, forbearance, kindness, goodness, faithfulness,*

Chapter VII: Invitation to be Infused by the Holy Spirit: Two Distinct Works

31. Acts 19:6 When Paul placed his hands on them, the Holy Spirit came on them, and they spoke in tongues and prophesied.

32. **Acts 1:8** *But you will receive power when the Holy Spirit comes on you; and you will be my witnesses in Jerusalem, and in all Judea and Samaria, and to the ends of the earth*

33. **Acts 2:14** *Then Peter stood up with the Eleven, raised his voice and addressed the crowd: "Fellow Jews and all of you who live in Jerusalem, let me explain this to you; listen carefully to what I say.*

34. **Romans 15:18** *I will not venture to speak of anything except what Christ has accomplished through me in leading the Gentiles to obey God by what I have said and done*

35. **2 Corinthians 5:17** Therefore, if anyone is in Christ, the new creation has come: The old has gone, the new is here!

36. **John 20:23** If you forgive anyone's sins, their sins are forgiven; if you do not forgive them, they are not forgiven."

37. **Acts 2:4** *All of them were filled with the Holy Spirit and began to speak in other tongues as the Spirit enabled them.*

38. **Acts 10:38** *how God anointed Jesus of Nazareth with the Holy Spirit and power, and how he went around doing good and healing all who were under the power of the devil, because God was with him.*

39. **Luke 4:1,18** 1Jesus, full of the Holy Spirit, left the Jordan and was led by the Spirit into the wilderness, … 18 "The Spirit of the Lord is on me, because he has anointed me to proclaim good news to the poor. He has sent me to proclaim freedom for the prisoners and recovery of sight for the blind, to set the oppressed free,

40. **Jeremiah 1:5** *"Before I formed you in the womb I knew you, before you were born I set you apart; I appointed you as a prophet to the nations."*

Notes

[1]Webb, Eugene. 2014. *The Christian Doctrine of the Trinity.* Columbia, MO: Uiversity of Missouri Press.

5*Greek-English Lexicon of the New Testament and Other Early Christian Literature.* 3rd Edition. University of Chicago Press.

[7]Ibid., 5

[13]Armstrong, Herbert W. 1985. *Mystery of the Ages.* New York: Dood, Mead and Company.